Journeys

Gary Meller

Chaplain Gary

Eph. 2:10

Note for Librarians: A cataloguing record for this book is available from Library and Archives Canada at www.collectionscanada.ca/amicus/index-e.html
ISBN 1-4120-7822-9

Printed in Victoria, BC, Canada. Printed on paper with minimum 30% recycled fibre. Trafford's print shop runs on "green energy" from solar, wind and other environmentally-friendly power sources.

PUBLISHING™

Offices in Canada, USA, Ireland and UK
This book was published *on-demand* in cooperation with Trafford Publishing. On-demand publishing is a unique process and service of making a book available for retail sale to the public taking advantage of on-demand manufacturing and Internet marketing. On-demand publishing includes promotions, retail sales, manufacturing, order fulfilment, accounting and collecting royalties on behalf of the author.

Book sales for North America and international:
Trafford Publishing, 6E–2333 Government St.,
Victoria, BC V8T 4P4 CANADA
phone 250 383 6864 (toll-free 1 888 232 4444)
fax 250 383 6804; email to orders@trafford.com
Book sales in Europe:
Trafford Publishing (UK) Limited, 9 Park End Street, 2nd Floor
Oxford, UK OXI IHH UNITED KINGDOM
phone 44 (0)1865 722 113 (local rate 0845 230 9601)
facsimile 44 (0)1865 722 868; info.uk@trafford.com
Order online at:
trafford.com/05-2720

10 9 8 7 6 5 4 3 2

TABLE OF CONTENTS

Dedication

Dedicated to my wife, Judy, and my daughter,
Toni. Thank you for your encouragement and
reviewing of the poems.
Special thanks to Pastor Steve Geyer, love ya, Bro.

Foreword

In June of 1998, after much prayer and confirmation by the Spirit, I decided to leave my job as a computer programmer and enter into training and pursue a ministry opportunity in Chaplaincy or where ever God led.

Part of the training program was to take a close look at myself to begin to understand what things in my life shape the way I respond and relate to others in crisis situations. Having been raised in a family where the "touchy-feely" emotions were seldom displayed, I was not looking forward to self-analysis. In God's infinite wisdom, He made sure I didn't understand the depth of this portion of the experience until I was committed to the program because He knew I would most likely have backed out and I would have lost a wonderful calling due to fear of the unknown.

As I began the process of looking at what things made me, me, I was faced with a real challenge. A hospice home care chaplain gave a presentation one day on poetry. God began to work in my heart and as a result of working through that first writing He began showing me how He could use my creative process to encourage and comfort others.

The things I write about all come from experiences I have had while working as a chaplain. My prayer is that as you read these poems you will remember these are moments from the lives of real people. I also pray that you will see the hope of the Lord woven into the fabric of each story. God's grace is present and sufficient in all things. God's touch occurs in the joy of the Good News as well as in prayers of a nurse at the bed of a dying man who has no family and shopping even with elderly parents for underwear.

Chapter 1
It Happened at the Hospital

The following poems reflect experiences I have had and people I have met while ministering as a Chaplain in a large regional medical center.

I've been given the privilege of laughing and crying with health care workers and have found that at times hope and refreshing can be found in a pan of Mrs. "M's" brownies or a box of cookies.

These poems are all based on those experiences and reflect some of the wonderful, caring nurses, patients and families I have the privilege of working with on a daily basis.

I could not include everyone but I did want you to see why I call these folks my heroes.

I have seen God's love displayed every day by these "Compassionate Angels" in blue scrubs.

I have been with these wonderful professionals when patients have died and have offered prayers as they cried for the loss of a valued life. In a moment they collect themselves because its time to move on to "The Next Thing."

Called often to minister in a hospice unit I have learned much about living. My conversations with friends who minister love and care as nurses in hospice taught me that while they are professionals doing a job, people often don't understand, there is more depth to each one than their role of "Hospice Nurse."

I have been called to units at times when a patient is dying and "No Family" can be found to be with the patient at that moment of passing.   For many of my heroes, they do all they can so the patient won't die alone.

If the words of these stories touch your heart please offer a prayer for the nurses, health care professionals and, yes, the Chaplains too that serve the medical needs in your area.

Compassionate Angel

For her life there is no hope, yet death holds no fears,
Still your care for this woman moves you to tears.

Her daughters have gathered,
they've said their good-byes,
You've answered their questions,
except for the "Whys?".

Compassionate Angel dressed all in blue,
Why are your tears falling like dew?
You manage life and meet death in the I.C.U.
What is it about this one that touches you?

Your compassion is evident
as you move around the bed,
Adjusting the pillow while
stroking her head.
The next few minutes
are the ones you always dread,
Her heart will stop and
death will replace life in this bed.

Compassionate Angel dressed all in blue,
Why are your tears falling like dew?
You manage life and meet death in the I.C.U.
What is it about this one that touches you?

As you continue your work,
you whisper a prayer,
You remove the needles
with tenderness and care.

You adjust her gown so her shoulders aren't bare,
If you had a comb, you'd straighten her hair.

Compassionate Angel dressed all in blue,
Why are your tears falling like dew?
You manage life and meet death in the I.C.U.
What is it about this one that touches you?

Telling the family is always the hard part to do,
You ask them for questions, they have one or two.
As they leave there's a moment of quiet just for you,
Then back to the unit 'til your shift is through.

Compassionate Angel dressed all in blue,
Why are your tears falling like dew?
You manage life and meet death in the I.C.U.
What is it about this one that touches you?

The Next Thing

A person of value is entrusted to my care.
A daughter says mom always had beautiful hair.

Over the hours and days she enters my heart;
Too soon, it seems, comes her time to depart.

I care for her and must say when she dies
I exit her room and wipe tears from my eyes.

For years I've cared but still there's death's sting.
I want to grieve but there's always the next thing.

There are papers to complete and forms to fill;
One patient needs help and another, their pill.

I say good-byes to the family, giving pats and a hug,
Then pause to find comfort and solace in my mug.

Sometimes, no matter how hard I try
I must slip away and have a brief cry.

The tears help to clear grief in my heart and my head;
Then comes the question, "Do you have one more bed?"

For years I've cared but still there's death's sting.
I want to grieve but there's always the next thing.

Midwives

Births and deaths mark such opposite extremes
each quite special but interchangeable it seems

The body prepares for the monumental event
Yet seems unprepared for the total energy spent

"I've never done this before, help me," some say,
Births or deaths we desire someone to show the way

Midwives at births are long proven as true;
Midwives in deaths are appropriate too.

In birth they care for the one bringing forth life,
In death for the spirit at the closing of life.

In birth and death we struggle for release.
The midwives give knowledge, care and peace.

In birth the child struggles to be freed from womb
In death the body struggles allowing the spirit to zoom

Midwives at births provide loving care;
at deaths, a loving presence to share.

There are times when they are the only ones there
to tend to the body and offer up prayer.

God, you are the giver of true spirit and life.
Thank you for your gift of the soul's midwife.

Hospice Nurse

Daily from compassion's well into your cup I pour
I am your hospice nurse, but know I'm so much more

I live in your community and sit by you in church
I serve you in days when for life's meaning you
search

I listened as you shared about your grandson running
track
It reminds me of my son who's bravely serving in Iraq

Daily from compassion's well into your cup I pour
I am your hospice nurse, but know I'm so much more

Please don't ask about your friend, if he's on my floor
Ask about my golf game or the sunrise o'er the shore

I walk a sacred path with patients and families too
My family time is precious and it helps me to renew

Daily from compassion's well into your cup I pour
I am your hospice nurse, but know I'm so much more

I enjoy when we laugh or just visit friend to friend
Thanks for asking about "me" and not about life's end

I gladly serve; it's what God's called me for
as from compassion's well into your cup I pour

I am a hospice nurse, now you know I'm so much
more

No Family

I prayed as I walked through the long darkened hall.
I opened the door to find no family at all.

A nurse kneeled beside him, smoothing hairs on his head.
"Come quickly!" He's dying; a prayer should be said.

I asked her his name and if he was a friend.
We just met, and he won't be alone at the end.

No family was listed, no next of kin name.
He listed a Pastor, but it's just not the same.

Where had he come from, where had he been?
What we knew of his past was his name, Glenn.

Though he passed from this world mostly alone,
with rejoicing arrives at the foot of God's throne.

When I think of the loneliness etched on his face
I 'm reminded of the wonder of God's saving grace.

He died without family and no long time friend,
But with the angels in heaven, eternity he'll spend.

Eight Years Old

He sits at a table with crayon in hand;
Is he drawing his home or a distant land?

He frames the page with particular care.
He pauses a moment, his eyes in a stare.

He selects a new color with an artist's flare;
He draws a person, then two, it's a pair.

He draws in a child, then another, for two;
Pink for the girl, for the boy, it's blue.

I watch and I wonder is it hope or loss?
The answer begins as he adds a brown cross.

To the cross he adds nails, then a body and head;
From the wounds he adds flows of crimson and red.

I wonder the meaning of this picture's part
And watch, fascinated, as he draws the Lord's heart.

He finishes by adding a house with a walk;
He's going to see Mom, there's no time to talk.

When asked of his meaning he explains with sincerity,
"We're all in God's family, the heart just adds clarity."

This child of eight, who, too soon lost his mother,
Now strengthens his Dad as they rely on each other.

Baby No Name

"Come quickly," said the voice, "a baby needs a blessing."
Its 1:00 A.M., I clear my head and try to finish dressing.

Mom holds her boy the rocking is slow;
Dad looks on but no emotions show.

Eight pounds plus, ten fingers, ten toes,
Their look asks "Why?" But only heaven knows.

By what name should I call him when the blessing is done?
They look, shrug their shoulders and say, "we don't have
one."

We were expecting a daughter and would have counted it
a joy.
We really do not have a name to fit this handsome baby
boy.

They seem content to let things continue in this way;
It's hard for me to bless this boy without a name to say.

We bless him in the name of the Father, Son and Spirit.
He passed from life to death yet never had to fear it.

Thank you for the parents that brought forth this baby boy;
We release him to Your care and count his presence joy.

You are a Loving Father who loves us each the same.
This baby you call a "Blessing", and there is no better
name.

May his parents hear his laughter and never feel shame.
For their boy is known in heaven, though on earth he had
no name.

Chapter 2
Senior Moments

I am a lover of history of all types and kinds, stuff that's true and the stuff in our minds.

I've had the privilege of serving for brief periods of time in long term care facilities where I met some of God's most precious creations.

As one gentleman told me, "Old age ain't for sissies but it's nothing to fear either."

Being the child of an aging parent ain't for sissies either as demonstrated by my friend Kim's experience of taking her parents shopping for "New Underwear."

I met a wonderful lady who referred to herself as "This Old Bag" who shared that at an age when most people think they have nothing to do God gave her a mission and purpose for her life.

One of the true gifts I received while ministering to those with dementia was to see first hand how God touches people even when they seem to be beyond reach to those who love them.

As I visited with one little lady I learned that if you listen you can hear the "Snow Talk."

At times people knew they were "Going Home" and would share with me what they were seeing beyond the veil.

New Underwear

As I drove up, Dad danced out with a flare.
"See ya later, I'm going to get new underwear."

It had been quite a week and this was one thing more.
It would be easier to leave Dad home and go to the store.

I stop for a moment and look but Dad's not there.
I hear his voice across the store, "I found my underwear!"

Mom is with me, riding in her little granny go-cart.
She hears him too, but just says, "Well, bless his heart."

I make a mistake of saying, "I need a pair to add to my stash."
Mom yells, "let's go!" Moments later I hear the crash.

Mom drove to the "Secrets" place as fast as she was able.
She made it through the door but upset a sales table.

She rummaged through the piles that were before her there
I tried to straighten things but felt the manager's stare.

She smiled as she said loud enough for everyone to share;
"Hey! They have your size, 100% cotton white underwear."

As I paid for my purchase, gave the money to the clerk,
I thought, "If my mom wasn't here I could call her a jerk."

As I drove off, I saw Dad dance with a flare
As he proudly showed everyone his new underwear.

Whose Grandma Are You?

Though her eyesight has faded her eyes twinkle blue.
I tell her my name but she asks, "Who are you?"

The housecoat is flowered and bright like the sun.
Every time that I see her it's always this one.

To find part of her story was my game plan.
We just sit and she smiles while holding my hand.

Her hand now is gnarled; the stroke's done its harm.
She smiles and says softly, "Your hand is so warm."

God gives just a moment of His wonderful grace.
I kneel; she smiles, then strokes my bearded face

Does she see her son, her husband or maybe her dad?
The moment soon passes with a sigh, sounding sad.

She looks out the window, I think towards a tree.
Whose face is that? She giggles, "Oh, it's me."

Though her eyesight has faded her eyes twinkle blue.
I tell her my name but she asks, "Who are you?"

Going Home

Are we home yet, how much longer must I wait?
Are we home yet, I think I hear Grandma calling from the gate.

I look up towards the ceiling, they think it's a stare.
The beautiful lady has come and is floating in the air.

I close my eyes and I can see her again.
An ageless face, is she family or friend?

Her clothing is shining white and flows on the air.
"You're safe with me," she whispers, "Come, I'll lead you there."

Are we home yet, how much longer must I wait?
Are we home yet, I think I hear Grandma calling from the gate.

A childhood memory or the desires of a failing heart.
Is this how a life must end or the glory of how one starts?

I hear those around me crying as they say good-bye.
I wish they knew the peace I have, even as I die.

I breathe deep the scent of honeysuckle and of roses.
Like looking through a window, now the curtain closes.

Are we home yet, how much longer must I wait?
Are we home yet, I think I hear Grandma calling from the gate.

I step from this world and my body is transformed
The missing limb and failing heart have been reformed.

I stand in white among the many, but yet we are as one.

The voice I've known but never heard says, "Welcome home, son."

In an instance all is perfected, all is right.
What I could never see, I now behold with perfect sight.

Are we home yet, how much longer must I wait?
Are we home yet, I think I hear Grandma calling from the gate.

Yes, I am home, no longer must I wait.
Yes, I am home, I hear Jesus calling from the gate.

Mom's Good-Bye

I stopped to visit her as I had for the last
few days. As I looked in her room, I saw she
had family with her and I was glad because she
has been alone for so many days without those
she loves.

I eavesdropped for just a moment as I watched
this young man cry as he stroked what was left
of her white hair and I saw the tears splash on
her cheek as he kissed her good bye.

As this scene has come back to me over the
days, I have come to believe her words may have
been as follows:

I know you can only stay for a few minutes, but
please come in.

Please, sit here by me.

I know I don't look the same as the last time
you saw me, but I'm still the same person
inside.

Yes, I do look funny without my teeth, but I've
lost too much weight to keep them in.

No, you won't cause me pain if you hold my hand
while you visit.

Tell me how you are doing. How is your family?

I remember when I would stroke your head when
you were ill, now the roles have changed.
Please don't stop.

My Pastor was here today and read "Psalm 23"
and prayed for me, it was such a comfort.

Yes, I know you love me and I know this is the hardest thing you have had to do.

Your tears don't bother me, I know you are hurting.

It's okay, she's my nurse.

You don't need to leave the room; she's just being my mother hen.

Thank you for stopping, I wish we had more time.

I'll miss you too, but there will come a time when we will sing together, dance together, be together again.

Snow Talk

Snowflakes are falling framed by skies gray.
The flakes may be speaking, shhh! What do they say?

I come beside her and kneel by her chair.
Through the window we watch, perhaps even stare.

Falling, dancing and prancing as they move from sky to ground.
So many shapes, no two the same, some square but none round.

Snowflakes are falling framed by skies gray.
The flakes may be speaking, shhh! What do they say?

Falling and covering pine boughs light over dark.
Her eyes begin to twinkle, a child's memory, a fresh spark.

What do you hear? Smiling slowly, crinkling her chin
She may hear the question but her response is a grin.

Snowflakes are falling framed by skies gray.
The flakes may be speaking, shhh! What do they say?

She says, "I think they are telling each other to behave;
It's hard to hear them, but I think that's what they say."

This Old Bag

Johanna will soon be 100 years old.
"Talk to her now!" by her sister I'm told.

Johanna sat straight in her chair without sag,
"How nice you would want to visit this Old Bag."

She said of her Christian family she'd been blessed.
Though having had struggles, God passed every test.

She was single 'til forty, some thought that quite odd,
Then she married a preacher, a man fully of God.

They had many years in ministry, but suddenly he died.
Arrangements were made, he was buried, she cried.

The tears weren't from anger, from the loss of a life,
They flowed from the aloneness of this widow, once wife.

When she was 97, she took a hard fall;
As she lay on the floor God placed a new call.

"When they come to see you and visit your place,
Tell them all how you've experienced My saving grace."

I asked her, "Through all of your years, of what would you brag?"
Her eyes sparkled as she said, "God's still using this Old Bag."

"Share this story with others so their faith may not lag,
Remind them of the day you met This Old Bag."

Chapter 3
Gifts, Prayers and Remembrances

The Lord has been gracious and often blessed me richly as I visited patients and families.

I walked into one room and there was a patient and her husband reading scripture and being close. As I excused myself for interrupting them the lady woke and told me about the picnic they had just been on. She described in detail the sounds and sights as they sat beside the "Water." She seemed a bit embarrassed when she realized that it was a dream. As we talked about her experience she came to hold that dream as one of God's touch points of Grace.

I have come to know some remarkable men of God over the years and I have found that behind many successful pastors stands a Godly woman known as the "Pastor's Wife." A pastor I met while he was a resident in a nursing home told me about how he missed his bride of many years when she died. Their story was the inspiration for "A Pretty Good Wife."

I was visiting with a friend one afternoon at work and she began to tell me how much she missed her dad who had died the previous year. She talked about how she still grieved and looked for ways to remember. She talked about the last Christmas gift that she had given her dad while he was in a nursing home. She told me she found it still in the box when they cleaned out his room a short while later and how she still keeps the remembrance that was her "Dad's Flannel Shirt."

I was called to see an uncle of mine who was dying at home from cancer. I had not seen this uncle for several years, but when I turned in the driveway memories from my childhood flooded back as I stopped the car and studied "The House by the River."

When my father-in-law died I was given the privilege and challenge of conducting his funeral. Ed was a bit of a legend in local music circles as he had a radio program for years where he would sing the old songs, mostly the westerns, but he always closed with a hymn. As we gathered in the church that day we were grieving our loss but we were celebrating that "Another of God's Singers Went Home."

I believe that God still does miracles today. Sometimes we find the extraordinary in the ordinary things like "Steeples and Streetlights." At other times, God may send you "Angels and Miracles."

I find that forgiveness is one of God's greatest healing miracles. I often thank God "For Giving Forgiving."

The death of a child is one of the most trying things a parent can go through and for those who are part of that special relationship of "Mothers and Sons" you know that when a child is buried, your wish may be to keep the child warm with a "Blanket of White."

Water

The water flows in silence yet sparkles like jewels of grace.
In the beauty of this moment I am sure I glimpse God's
face.
The solace that it brings to me is way beyond compare;
For in my dream you're with me and share the moments
there.

When I awoke I felt confused and oh, so much alone.
It's just water pouring in a glass, not waves upon a stone.

To the woman, Jesus said, "I will give you water that is
living."
As I battle my disease I am thankful for His Love and
giving .

The water flows in silence yet sparkles like jewels of grace.
In the beauty of this moment I am sure I glimpse God's
face.
The solace that it brings to me is way beyond compare;
For in my dream you're with me and share the moments
there.

In green pastures we will rest in the willow's shadows cool;
Beside the quiet waters I'll meet Jesus, and we'll linger at a
pool.

As I share fears and dreams with this man from Galilee
He listens and says, "Daughter, cast your burdens upon
me."

The water flows in silence yet sparkles like jewels of grace.
In the beauty of this moment I am sure I glimpse God's
face.

The solace that it brings to me is way beyond compare;
For in my dream you're with me and share the moments
there.

Now my heart cries out, "Lord, I know I'll be fine,
But my tears are for the loved ones that I will leave
behind."

My Savior will calm their fears and all their needs fulfill.
Wind-tossed waves turn calm as glass, when He says,
"Peace, be still."

The water flows in silence yet sparkles like jewels of grace.
In the beauty of this moment I am sure I glimpse God's
face.
The solace that it brings to me is way beyond compare;
For in my dream you're with me and share the moments
there.

The Pastor's Wife

She cares for her husband when wounded by strife;
She married the church, she's the Pastor's wife.

She must be a champion for all who request her prayer;
She must have her head in heaven without her nose in the air.

She must be open and friendly to all that are new
And be sure not to ignore old Mrs. You-know who.

She must wear just enough makeup to highlight her face;
If she wears too much she'll be corrected, with Grace?

She meets with a Mom, "Help my child", she pleads,
While alone she cries for her own unmet needs.

Pastor's wives can come in any old size;
The thing that they share is Christ in their eyes.

Their husbands are called for their talents and skill;
The wives provide the balance, the voice small and still.

As they move from church to church and parish to parish
She makes new friends, but it's the old ones she'll cherish.

"Genesis" says it's not good for man to be alone,
So the perfect completer came from a hunk of bone.

Pastors are better when equipped with a spouse,
They're granted the grace to make a home of God's House.

She cares for her husband when wounded by strife;
She married the church, she's the Pastor's wife.

A Pretty Good Wife

Mae was a pretty good wife
My partner for years in ministry and life

She went to heaven, that sweet by and by
She left in the night without saying good-bye

My wife left me, she just up and went
Now here I am sitting without a cent

I know she's enjoying God's presence and more
But I'm stuck down here feeling lonesome and poor

Mae was a pretty good wife
My partner for years in ministry and life

I'd preach with my heart 'til the rafters would ring
She'd play the piano; brother, could she sing!

She gave me good sons, numbering four
We raised them right here, just up the North Shore

We were married 53 years, that's not a bad start
I know that she left, but she still fills my heart

Mae was a pretty good wife
My partner for years in ministry and life

Yes, Mae was a pretty good wife

Dad's Flannel Shirt

I can look back now without the tears and hurt
And smile as I think of Dad's old flannel shirt.

The few years were very difficult,
even though it wasn't his fault.

He said the nursing home made him feel old,
He had trouble getting around and was always cold.

We bought him the shirt for some special day.
I don't remember, was it Christmas or his birthday?

We found it neatly folded away when he died.
The worn collar reminded me of him, and I cried.

As we drove to the cemetery, this thought in my head,
"Dad would be warm in his shirt", though I knew he was dead.

Though it's been several years Dad's in my heart and head.
That old flannel shirt still hangs on the post of my bed.

It brings comfort, support and yet a tear or two.
But I know its Dad saying, "I'm still with you."

I can look back now without the tears and hurt
And smile as I think of Dad's old flannel shirt.

I still thank God for that old flannel shirt.

House by the River

As I turned and went up the drive, in my mind's eye I could see
childhood memories of girl cousins, and Ivan and Marie

The river flows slowly and bends near the drive
the ice is now going soon spring will arrive

In the winter ice was harvested and stored with a scheme
turned with cream and salt it soon yields ice cream

I remember old yellow buses that were great places to hide
and homemade doodle bugs and being too young to ride

The place seemed to look just the same as it did years before,
missing were spotted cows and short-legged dogs by the score

I'm not sure what to expect as I knock on the door
but there comes a bark and a short-legged dog, just as before

The kitchen would yield rhubarb sauce over fresh yellow cake
I seem to remember venison gravy and a hearty pancake

The place may never have been the grand Taj Mahal
but the coffee was hot and the open door welcomed all

Ivan could crinkle his head and waggle his ears
it's amazing what you remember after all these years

As I left and went down the drive, in my mind's eye I could see
childhood memories of girl cousins, and Ivan and Marie

Another of God's Singers Went Home

Another of God's singers went home
Another line added to life's perfect poem

The author of life is penning the lines
Like rustling of wind in the whispering pines

Years write the verses and faith the refrains
Forgiveness brings white to old crimson stains

Another of God's singers went home
Another line added to life's perfect poem

Harmony and Melody make the song whole
God breathed life in his body and hope in his soul

The lyrics of his life were set to three-four time
He touched many lives even long after his prime

Another of God's singers went home
Another line added to life's perfect poem

Family and friends will miss the music of his life
He loved his family and was devoted to his wife

God's Word says that though we die we are not dead
So it isn't good-bye it's Toodle-li-do to you Ed

Another of God's singers went home
Another line added to life's perfect poem

Yes, Another of God's singers went home

Steeples and Streetlights

I was standing on the sidewalk just waiting for my ride
She approached me from a distance but stopped by my side.

She took a drag on her cigarette and her story she did share.
She seemed to me a gentle one as we shared the morning air.

It's been a really bad week, so please don't think me odd.
As I was praying here last night I believe I heard from God.

My Dad is ill with cancer and I couldn't bear the loss
As I stood here on the sidewalk, just staring at that cross.

I asked the Father for a sign before my Dad is gone.
As I began to pray here that streetlight just came on.

I bared my soul and shared my heart with the Holy One;
Please let there be a better time before his life is done.

As soon as I had said "Amen", the streetlight just went off.
She took another drag and I waited as she coughed.

Thank you, sir, for listening and please don't think me odd.
I knew that I must share with you just how I heard from God.

I thanked her as she finished and continued on her walk.
I looked to heaven as I said "God, we need to talk."

Thank you, Lord, for reminding me of just who's in control.
In this case, being present was the purpose of my role.

Angels and Miracles

I entered the room not knowing the need
The pain on their faces was easy to read.

We are believers, our trust is in Jesus
Thank you for coming, taking time just for us

The cancer has now moved to his back
We're looking for prayer to keep us on track

She shared the story of where they had walked
He nodded in agreement as she cried and talked

When he did speak, he began with a joke
His humor was so bad I thought I would choke

We shared and laughed but time too quickly sped away
Then we agreed that it was time to focus and pray

Prayer was needed for his swelling hand and painful back
Please ask God to heal and increase the faith we may lack

The next time I visited there was a difference in the room
A lightness and joy had dispelled the night's gloom

He waved from his bed as he was too weak to stand
What looked like a baseball was now clearly a hand

There were fingers and knuckles and it bent at the wrist
As he waved and smiled my eyes filled with mist

Their doctor agreed it was a miraculous story
And the couple continued to give God the glory

They called me their angel but I'm just a man
Who struggles with praise when I know its God's plan

So I thank you Jesus for the gift of healing
And thanks too Lord for angels in prayer, kneeling.

Stranger in the House

A STRANGER MOVED INTO THE HOUSE RECENTLY
SHE WAS SMALL, QUIET AND AWFULLY HARD TO SEE

WE KNEW SOMETHING WAS WRONG, THERE WERE
THINGS OUT OF PLACE
WE THOUGHT ABOUT WHAT COULD BE WRONG, BUT
FOUND IT HARD TO TRACE

PICTURES AND SCANS WERE ORDERED TO FIND THE
STRANGER'S LAIR
WHEN HER HIDING PLACE WAS FOUND, WE THREW
HER OUT OF THERE

A SEARCH WAS MADE AGAIN TO BE SURE SHE'D
REALLY GONE
THEN CAME THE AWAKENING THAT THIS WOULD
DRAG ALONG

MORE CLEANING OF THE HIDING PLACE WAS SAID TO
REQUIRE
SOME RADIATION TO BE USED TO REND HER OUT LIKE
FIRE

THE GOOD NEWS IS WE FOUND HER BEFORE SHE
COULD UNPACK
THROUGHOUT THIS TIME WE HAVE FOUND A GRACE
THAT DOES NOT LACK

THE STRANGER'S NAME IS CANCER, A WORD THAT'S
HARD TO SWALLOW
BY GOD'S GRACE WE HAVE FOUND IN SELF-PITY WE
NEED NOT WALLOW

I MUST TO ALL CONFESS AND TO EACH ONE TELL
WE FOUND THAT GOD IS MIGHTIER THAN A CELL

The Lighthouse

Jesus said, "I am the Way, the Truth and the Light."
But I can lose those words in a storm at night.

My ship is battered as I attempt to stay my course
My fears come like winds driven by a hurricane force.

I search through the night for a port of safe refuge
As I wallow in darkness, small fears become huge.

I long for my family but they are far from my sight.
I pray and hear the words, "Steer towards my Light."

I search the horizon as I crest a large wave.
In my doubts I wonder does God really save?

I see the beacon's flash and know I've beaten this storm
As I study this vision, the lighthouse takes form.

Jesus, you are the Way, the Truth and the Light
Forgive me my doubts in the storm of the night.

Jesus said, "Even in darkness you're not gone from my sight.
When you doubt I am with you, I'll send my beacon, my Light."

Mothers and Sons

Two Mothers and two Sons;
Two lives with much left undone.

Brian and Zachary each had a name;
Two hearts broken, but who's to blame?

Humor given as their personality's strong suit;
For each, living life was their great pursuit.

Zach pursued hunting, fishing and the outdoors look.
Brian was the wonderful son, athlete and cook.

What would they accomplish, what would they be?
The loss of these sons, neither Mom could foresee.

Two Mothers and two Sons;
Two lives with much left undone.

Two Sons and two Mothers;
Two hearts missing the promise of another.

Who would they love; whom would they marry?
The questions cry out but the silence is scary.

The empty days often put you to the test;
But in our eyes, Mom, you two were the best.

We both understand the separation feels odd:
Mom, hear what we say, we're safe, home with God.

Jesus wants me for a sunbeam, the old song does say;
Our love shines for you still in the sunrise each day.

Two Mothers and two Sons;
Two lives with much left undone.

A Father's PSALM

For months I waited, thanking God for your arrival
Now I kneel to plead and pray for your survival

As the last hours approached I was filled with emotion
Your mommy sang to you but you made not a motion

I watch and I pray as for your delivery they prepare
I've never met you in life but oh how I care, God knows
how I care

There's no crying, the nurse says, "She's stillborn."
I want to celebrate because even though you died, you're
still born

Wrapped in a blanket you're brought to mom's room
Now I see why she smiled as you grew in her womb

You'll never cuddle and fall asleep on my chest
You've gone to the Father; in you, darling, He got the best

The joyful future I planned has now darkened with gloom
I'm surprised at golden light that now showers the room

I cry and my tears fall on you my dear wee lass
Jesus reminds me that this pain too, will pass

I pray and search for some peace in my mind
I close my eyes and this picture I find

You crawl up on Jesus and place your head on His chest
You've gone home to the Father so in peace you can rest

You've gone home to the Father and in you we've been
blest
Yes, you've gone home to the Father and in you we've
been blest.

BLANKET OF WHITE

The earth is open
Looking dark and cold

My heart now is empty
My heartache untold

The grave is now enclosing
Him now forever to hold

Held in my heart but gone from my sight
The snow now covers like a woolen blanket of white.

As trees slumber in winter
Then in spring bloom bright

So you too now slumber gone from my sight
While in heaven you'll dance in garments of white.

For Giving Forgiving

I Thank you Lord
> For Giving
>> Healing and health
>> Provision and wealth

> For giving
>> Plant and beast
>> Harvest and feast

> For giving
>> Birth and life
>> New Birth and new life

> For giving
>> Jesus
>> Jesus

I thank you Lord
> For Forgiving
>> My wasted time
>> When opportunities were prime

> For Forgiving
>> My words of hate
>> That Shattered hearts like broken plates

> For Forgiving
>> What my eyes did see
>> Peeking where I should not be

> For Forgiving
>> Those who are at a loss
>> To find value in Christ on the cross

I thank you Lord for Giving, Forgiving.